THE RETIREMENT BOOK

Written By:
Herbert Kavet

Illustrated By:
Martin Riskin

Manufactured in the United States of America

30 29 28 27 26 25 24 23 22 21 20 19 18 17 16 15 14 13 12 11 10 9 8 7 6 5

Ivory Tower Publishing Co., Inc.
111 Bauer Drive, Oakland, NJ 07436

INTRODUCTION

Now that you're retired, you probably have the time to read these stupid introductions and acknowledgment pages. Who knows? You might want to even peruse the table of contents that everyone else ignores. I bet you wondered what was written on all these pages, during those years when you were too busy to notice.

Well, I'll tell you. Mostly, I thank my aunt and uncles and wife for things like support and insights. But with a book for people of retirement age, whose memories are probably starting to rust a little, I'd like to remind you to

PAY FOR THIS BOOK!!

Marge was emptying out her desk and finally found that pile
of invoices that was missing since 1987.

Tony decided to try to make it home with the pens he'd been accumulating in his lower desk drawer.

EARLY BIRD SPECIALS

It's never too early to gear yourself up for Early Bird Specials as this daily event will be a central part of your retirement program. The secret to full utilization of Early Bird Specials is to wake up at a really early hour. By the time you are ready for retirement this should be absolutely no problem as you've probably been up with the birds for years.

The trick here though, once you're retired, is to eat breakfast shortly after you rise. This allows you to fit in lunch by maybe 10:00 or 10:30 and be raring to go for an Early Bird Special at 4:00 or 4:30.

"Some of these erasers may be of interest to the Smithsonian."

"Oh don't worry about the combination. We all found where you scratched it on the wall years ago."

"Tell us again how you did business before faxes and Federal Express."

HOW TO DRIVE LIKE A RETIRED PERSON

Wearing a hat is a good start, and really scrunching down in your seat will certainly let people know that you are probably a senior citizen. But the most important skill, once you retire, is to drive in the center of the road, straddling two lanes. Some retired people try to straddle three lanes, but only those with Winnebagos are even partially successful. Keeping in the center of the road gives you lots more time to react to emergencies coming at you from the sides, and lots more room for errors when taking curves at 20 miles per hour under the speed limit.

Speaking of speed, once you're retired, 55 M.P.H. will seem like a very reasonable speed at which to travel. You'll seldom get speeding tickets, and you'll never have your car towed for illegal parking.

It's time to retire when no one notices you dozing off during meetings.

It's time to retire when colleagues start sizing up your office.

It's time to retire when you're the only one they trust to be the designated driver.

It's time to retire when everyone wants you on their project team because you're the only one who really knows how to get things done.

It's time to retire when your files are making the floors sag,
and your rolodex is all filled.

SEEING LIKE A RETIRED PERSON

By the time you are ready for retirement, you are probably a pro at using your bifocals. Finding them or the reading glasses, once they've been put down someplace, is an entirely different matter. For many retired people, finding their glasses turns out to be a major midmorning activity. Reading menus that some artsy person printed in small maroon letters on a red background, in a restaurant that is illuminated by a jar of fireflies in the kitchen, is the dread of all retirees. Early Bird Specials were invented so retired people could get to a restaurant while there was still enough daylight available for them to read a menu. Once you are retired, it is entirely acceptable for you to demand a flashlight from the maitre d'.

It's time to retire when you're finally discovered as the mystery pen hoarder.

SEX AND RETIREMENT

You'll have lots more time to enjoy sex once you're retired. Unfortunately, at this point in your life, "getting a little action" means your prune juice is working rather than it's time for an afternoon roll in the hay. Before retirement, you may have awakened in the middle of the night for a little sex, but now, more likely it's to go to the toilet. While your biological urges may be slowing down, there is no harm in looking, and our more liberal society certainly gives you opportunities to do that. If you don't live near a beach, you can rent these videos that are best checked out when no one you know is hanging around the cash register counter. Many of the people you see milling about video stores in the afternoon are just waiting for a clear run at the cashier so they can get "Passion Cheerleaders Go To Dallas" home before their minister sees them.

It's time to retire when everyone has already heard all your jokes and stories.

It's time to retire when people you hired are "fast tracking" it right past you.

DRESSING LIKE A RETIRED PERSON
WOMEN

Retired women have the maturity to realize really good gifts are going to have to be bought by themselves.

Retired women still want to be stylish, but comfort is starting to take precedence over the latest fashions. They look forward to changing into something loose and comfy every time they come back from a shopping trip. Buying a bathing suit doesn't take three days any longer, 'cause they don't buy bathing suits.

DRESSING LIKE A RETIRED PERSON
MEN

Retired men don't worry too much about which tie width is in fashion this month. They have learned not to throw out the old ones (at least those without stains), 'cause they always come back in style. Mostly, retired men just don't wear ties. Retired men have pretty much adapted a style of dress they feel comfortable with, and people can go to hell if they don't like it.

It's time to retire when your frequent flyer miles will take you
to places you don't even <u>want</u> to visit.

It's time to retire when other employees have finally figured out some of your communication channels.

It's time to retire when you've been around so long that you know
for sure no new idea is going to work.

COMPUTERS & RETIREMENT

Some retired people buy computers to play with and to keep track of all the things they used to keep in their heads or on a slip or two of paper. Most retired people are relieved to have made it out of the business world before anyone noticed just how computer illiterate they were. Only a few years ago, many of these retirees thought "software" referred to some new comfy underwear; and they still have to get their grandchildren to program the VCR.

"Sam, could you leave me the name of your barber before you leave?"

"I've got this new system to help me remember."

"Oh, those must be all the slips of paper I wrote notes on and then forgot where I put them."

MEMORY–REMEMBERING YOU'RE RETIRED

This old, retired fellow was complaining to his cronies about how bad his memory had become. "Why just last night," he said, "I woke up at about 2 a.m. and felt rather aroused. So I asked my wife if she would like to have a little 'fun.' She told me we already had 'fun' at 11:30 and 1:00, and that she was tired and would like to get some sleep now. So I asked her, what did you say your name was?"

The real problem with memory, once you retire, is how it tires you out. You go upstairs for something and by the time you get to the top of the staircase, you forget what you went up there for. Some retired people spend entire days wandering from room to room trying to recall just what they were looking for. This, combined with finding your glasses, is already a full-time job.

Harry remembers when they used to drink at Christmas parties.

When you're ready to retire, all the women feel comfortable
flirting outrageously with you.

"When Frank retires, it's going to cut my commute by 15 minutes."

FITNESS AFTER RETIREMENT

You'll find that after retirement, you'll have time for all those healthy activities that you never could quite fit into your schedule while you were working. You'll also find that you hurt for three days after doing almost any of them. Exercise is great but you need a balance here. Your back and other parts will eventually stop functioning if you don't exercise to strengthen them, but the strengthening exercises are going to kill you. You can't win. Try joining a club. The memberships are quite inexpensive. They can afford these low prices because no one comes back after two visits.

"Margaret has enough sick leave accumulated to carry her
till October of the next century."

THE HEARTBURN & GAS DRAWER

Every person nearing retirement has a special drawer in their desk filled with indigestion and intestinal problem remedies. Antacid, hemorrhoidal and hair loss potions are only the front part of the drawer. The back part contains the "in-depth" cures.

Upon retiring, cleaning out this drawer is one of the most poignant final acts you will do. Most of the other people in the office have probably been using this drawer as an on-site HMO for years, and once you retire, they will be left without medical care. Thoughtful retirees pass a portion of the medical center on to the next retiree in line.

John beat the odds. He stayed computer illiterate until retirement.

"And leave a couple of hours to train Larry's replacement."

"Hey–there's no fighting over my parking space until <u>after</u> I'm gone."

GLOBAL WARMING EFFECT DOESN'T WARM YOU

It's time to retire when you're the only one freezing in the office. The kids are walking around outside in short sleeves and yet, you think gangrene is spreading in your feet, even with your sweater on. Women are different at this age. The women are all going through menopause and are sweating to death. This is why they put office thermometers behind those locked plastic boxes.

"I decided it was time to retire when the secretaries started kissing me on the forehead at the Christmas Party."

RETIRING TO WORK ON NOSE & EAR HAIRS

There may be no new signs of hair growth on the top of your head, but there is no stopping the ear and nose hairs which, like grass, come back multifold every time you cut them. Keeping these critters under control is a full-time job and no working man has the time to do it properly. Once you retire, of course, you probably will resign yourself to letting them grow wild since you're no longer going to be flirting with the young ladies at the office.

Men can never understand why the stuff grows wild all over their bodies but refuses to sprout on top of their heads.

"You can let it out now–she's not looking."

"But **WE** had to live overseas where our retirement dollar would go further."

RETIREMENT TRAVEL

Now you will have the time to visit all those places around the world where flush toilets, hot showers and potable drinking water have yet to be discovered. You can travel to these exotic, faraway locations on rickety, questionable airlines with names like Saudi Arab Airway, Uno Nigerian or Yugoslavian Airlines, and be exposed to diseases your doctor will be absolutely baffled by. One friend, and I am not making this up, returned from Africa and proceeded to lose every hair on his body. They never did figure that one out.

RETIREMENT TRAVEL

You can, of course, visit Europe, which is totally civilized and where your entire monthly Social Security Check will buy you a cup of cappuccino. Europe has no funny diseases but in exchange, they take all your money. Many retired people prefer to ride around their own country in a mobile home, which gives them an opportunity to screw up traffic across the width and breadth of the land, as well as publicizing all their favorite political and social causes on their bumpers.

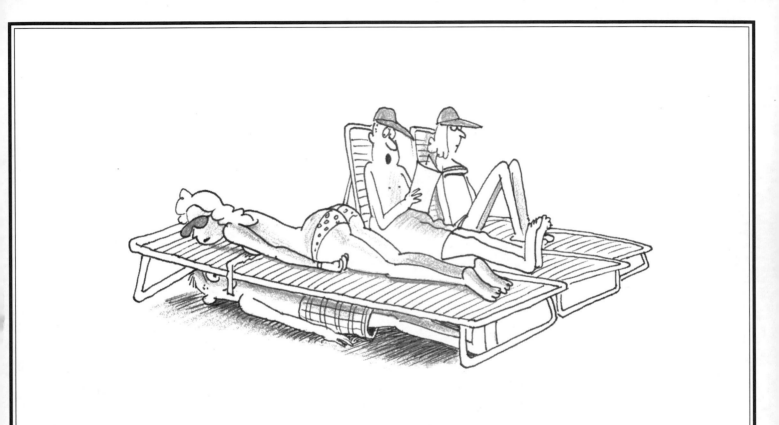

"I'm not sure Higglesworth has a mature enough attitude
for a retirement village."

"It's sunny here almost every day."

"I'm retired. I don't buy nuttin' that requires assembly!"

"When Bernie retires, he's going to feel the loss of income more from the football pools than his paycheck."

The directors learn what Sonya's vested interest in the profit sharing plan amounted to.

FINALLY, TIME TO GO TO THE BATHROOM

Now that you're retiring, you can look forward to your Saturday toilet regimen every day of the week. It will provide a wonderful opportunity to catch up on all those magazines you were going to read some day, and should go a long way towards solving those regularity problems you've been struggling with. Your spouse, of course, has to be willing to use the uncomfortable downstairs toilet.

Peabody accumulated so much vacation time that he almost went broke trying to use it.

"That was quite a dance you did at the retirement party."

"Once you retire, there'll be no one left to share liquid lunches with."

JUST WHEN YOU'VE LEARNED TO DO EVERYTHING, YOU RETIRE

You don't take crap from sales clerks and you can handle any emergency at work with aplomb. Heaven knows you've been there before and have seen all these problems dealt with over the years. One way you can really tell it's time to retire is when you hear yourself saying "We tried that once, but it didn't work." The rule is that each generation has to make their own mistakes or they can't grow up with any sense of accomplishment. I know, my kids insist on doing every dumb thing I ever did.

"I don't know whose going to match some of Victor's skills."

"Those guys in accounting just can't take a joke."

"Now that you mention it, these kids <u>DO</u> dress differently."

RETIRE AND TAKE CARE OF YOUR HAIR

Finally there is enough time to spend arranging your hair rather than just combing it. Your bathroom has an array of shampoos, conditioners, colorers, thickeners and tonics that are starting to rival the prescriptions that have already over-filled the drawers and medicine chest.

"They set the mandatory retirement age just high enough so they don't have the energy to struggle at the end."

RETIREMENT AND YOUR DIET

*Marcia found certain foods just weren't compatible
with her gastrointestinal system.*

By the time you are ready for your farewell banquet, you've developed a pretty good idea of what your gastrointestinal system likes and what it is likely to revolt over. You've probably developed the caution of a royal taster and try weird new foods with the suspicion learned by years of popping antacid tablets. You don't travel anywhere without a goodly supply of them in your pocket or purse. Make your bland preferences known for your retirement lunches early, leaving the raw, the incendiary, the unpronounceable and the natural for staff members under 30.

"We're going to really miss your cheese dip at the office parties."

"The office is really going to feel different once Martha retires."

"Janice is a free lance volunteer. She now does for nothing what she used to get paid for."

MORNING COFFEE

Changing your source of this life-giving elixir at this point in your life will take some getting used to. You may have been the only one who didn't know what they really were selling at the coffee wagon, but over the years, you grew to love the coffee. Now, thrown to your own devices, you or your spouse will have to learn to match the special taste only the coffee at work seems to have.

"Herman is having a tough time keeping busy since retirement."

"You realize, Russ, that when you retire, I'll be the only one
in the company that smokes."

AARP IN YOUR MAILBOX

Every mail order company in the country knows the instant you retire and will be trying to sell you something.

The volume of mail from AARP (American Associate of Retired Persons, in case you're a foreign reader—every retired person in the U.S. knows these initials better than their own) has been multiplying in your mailbox since you were 50, and now that you are actually retiring, it reaches a crescendo that causes hernias in mailmen. No other organization serves a group that has the time on their hands to read all their stuff, plus the money to buy the insurance, health and travel schemes offered. AARP mailings require a forest of trees the size of Oregon each week.

You find yourself on virtually every junk mail list. During the Christmas season, your mailman visits his chiropractor daily.

"Ralphie always knows when he's had enough to drink."

"Winslow, I know you're retired, but this is just delaying the game."

WAITING FOR THE MAIL

This is a splendid midday activity that most of your contemporary retirees have developed into a fine art to fill the hours between lunch (10:30) and dressing for the Early Bird Specials (3:15). Checking for the mail every few minutes during this period, will insure that all your AARP mailings, catalogs and bills will be in your hands at the earliest possible moment, and will reduce the chance of these valuable documents being stolen or lost. A short chat with the mailman will keep you up to date on neighborhood news and may just help tip you off as to which neighbors are receiving those "sexually oriented" catalogs.

"Madame, doggie bags are NOT permitted at the Early Bird Buffet."

"This all started when Gwen found out her cleaning lady was making more than her retirement package."

"Sometimes Bob stops to think and forgets to start again."

CHECKING IN WITH 800 PHONE NUMBERS

What a wonderful source of information and companionship these free phone calls provide. You can check on bank balances daily, chat with your broker, learn about the weather, double check every bill, discuss new food recipes and a host of other entertaining conversations at no cost whatsoever. On days when the mail arrives early or it's too rainy to walk to the mall, let these toll free electronic marvels be your own Disneyland.

"The retired guys are the ones who are freezing all the time."

"Now that you're retired, you can finally catch up on the Book of the Month Club commitment."

"You're going to expect lunch <u>every</u> day now?"

KEEPING UP WITH THE NEWS

Retirement is the period of your life where you have the time to keep totally up-to-date on the news. Modern communications make this an entertaining and easy fun-filled activity. One problem you will notice with the news is that the names of the countries these days are changing faster than anyone but a map maker cares to keep up with. To help you locate these new places, figure that if it ends in "IA" or "STAN," it's near Russia. Anything with weird combinations of vowels is probably Africa and countries that are totally unpronounceable go in Asia. With all these changes, it is comforting to know that the Atlantic and Pacific Oceans keep the turmoil and revolutions away from our shores.

"Your retirement's scheduled for next month, Ellsworth, unless you force me to move it up."

"Since you retired, everything's 'GOD WILLING.'"

"Now that Lionel is retired, he thinks 'Good in Bed' means sleeping through the night."

A LITTLE BUSINESS ON THE SIDE

Tom finally was able to put his job skills into use with a business of his own.

All those years filled with earning a living left you full of experience, but until now, little time to start an operation of your own. Once you've retired, you'll find yourself in tremendous demand as a highly paid consultant and expert. You might as well take advantage of this earning opportunity especially if they pay in cash, so it won't reduce your retirement benefits.

"So I told him, you're retired now with time on your hands,
find a hobby, find a pastime."

Being retired gave Selma lots more time to work on her gray hairs.

Being retired means never caring where your wife goes when she goes out, as long as you don't have to go with her.

IDENTIFYING THE MYSTERY OFFICE FARTER

As we get older, our digestive systems function less efficiently and certain foods or eating habits may generate a little gas. Around a big office, it is pretty easy for an experienced person to hide this problem by cleverly utilizing a slammed door or a clacking copy machine to mask the noise. The odor, of course, tends to hang around a bit and while your fellow workers may have been suspicious, proving your guilt was difficult.

Once you leave, however, they are going to realize the identity of the Mystery Office Farter and this is the main reason so few retirees come back to visit.

"No, I don't have any idea where your glasses are either."

(Tune–"The Farmer In The Dell")

We hate to see you go
We hate to see you go
We hope the heck you never come back
We hate to see you go

Camp Lokanda, Circa 1944